HOW TO BE A KNIGHT

Cover illustration: Lee Cosgrove

Edited by Lesley Sims
Consultant: Dr. Craig Taylor
With thanks to Timothy Duke at the College of Arms

Design: Stephen Wright and Mike Olley
Additional design: Matt Preston
Cover design: Stephen Moncrieff and Matt Preston

HOW TO BE A KNIGHT

Written by the most chivalrous
Sir Archibald Whistleblade
(also known as Sam Taplin)

Illustrated by a gracious draughtsman of the Antipodes,
Sir Basil Silvermoon
(also known as Ian McNee)

Contents

Chapter One
So you want to be a knight? — 7
Knights: a quick guide — 10
Chivalry — 14
Courtly love — 24
Where you fit in — 30

Chapter Two
Knight school — 33
Starting out — 34
Tonight's the knight — 42
Kitting yourself out — 46

Chapter Three
To battle! — 55
Battle tactics — 56
Raids — 64
Castle warfare — 66
Crazy crusades — 71

Chapter Four
Home for the knight — 78
Castle browsing — 79
Castle life — 86

Chapter Five
Tournaments and challenges — 92
Muddy mêlées — 94
Bone-jangling jousts — 98
Handy heralds — 102
Pas d'armes — 108

Chapter Six
Knight notes — 109
Knights to remember — 110
Your own coat of arms — 117
Index — 125

Chapter One
So you want to be a knight?

Have a look in the mirror...
Could you **rescue a damsel from a dungeon?**
Or **knock a warrior off his galloping horse?**
If you want to be a knight, the answers had better be **YES!**

Knights are the most **formidable warriors** in the medieval world (aka the **Middle Ages**), and it's not a job for cowards or puny weaklings. If you make it to the top, you can expect **fame**, **fortune** and **songs** about how wonderful you are. But it won't be easy.

Why be a knight?

Every time a knight rides into battle, he knows he might get killed. So **why choose such a dangerous career?**

One of the main reasons is this: **Everyone loves you.**

A knight in shining armour is the main man, the ruler of the roost. When you ride along a crowded street, all eyes are on you. Everyone cheers. Some might even applaud.

A successful knight is the **star of the show**, and that's why everyone is dying to be one. (Sometimes literally...)

Need another reason to become a knight? How about having a place reserved in heaven just for you? Fighting bravely can show what a good Christian you are. Courageous knights go all out to impress God, expecting to be rewarded when they, um, die.

Knights: a quick guide

You'll need lots of determination to succeed as a knight, but that's not all. Your shopping list will include:

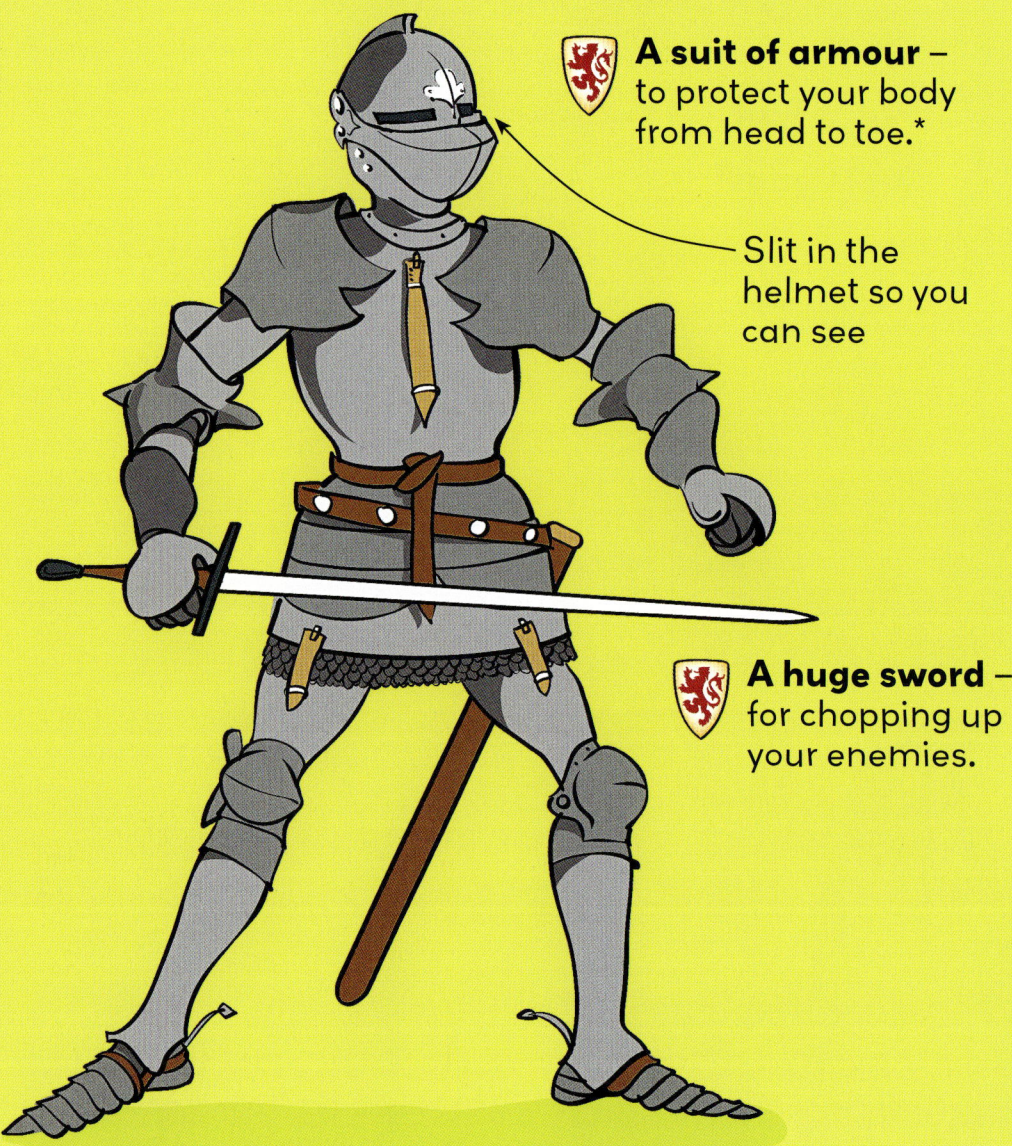

A suit of armour – to protect your body from head to toe.*

Slit in the helmet so you can see

A huge sword – for chopping up your enemies.

* The armour shown is for a 15th-century knight. If you're not up to date, you'll wear something else – see page 49.

 **No fewer than THREE horses...**

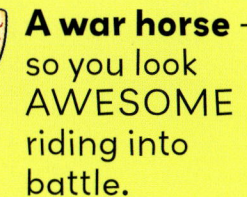 **A war horse** – so you look AWESOME riding into battle.

 A riding horse – to look EVEN MORE awesome, when trotting between castles.

 A baggage horse – because you can't look AT ALL awesome, carrying all your gear.

Home sweet home

Of course, none of this comes cheap. The armour will cost you more than most people earn in ten years, and your snorting, battle-trained war horse will be even more expensive.

And that's before you even think about building **a castle** to live in. So you'd better have rich parents (or find a rich lord to serve). One day, if you really make it big, you might own an estate like this one.

Your water mill for grinding grain

Your villagers farming the fields

Chivalry

Just as important as what you own is **how you behave**. Knights have to obey an incredibly strict set of rules, known together as **chivalry**.

The idea of chivalry really caught on in the twelfth century, when a bunch of lords in France began to follow a **code of conduct for warriors on horseback**. Since the French for horse is **cheval**, the code is known as **chivalry**, and there are **two main parts** to it.

1. Bravery

To be a proper knight – a "chivalrous" one – you must be **brave to the point of foolhardiness.** In fact, some people would say you have to be more than slightly crazy.

2. Honour

It's not enough to **risk your life** fighting against **impossible odds**; you also have to be **extremely fair and polite** while you're at it.

If you want your fellow knights to respect you, always act with **honour**. This is what makes knights different from other warriors, with their rude, cheating ways.

A few rules to remember:

NEVER...

...run away from the enemy.

...attack an unarmed enemy, or attack from behind.

Nice to have a little break from all the fighting...

...abandon a friend.

I've just remembered – I forgot to feed my horse... Bye!

ALWAYS...

...**defend innocent people** who can't defend themselves.

"Don't even think of attacking them!"

...**spare an enemy knight's life if he surrenders.** (Obviously, this is about honour. But it can also be about making loads of money if you sell the knight back to his lord for a whopping great price.)

...treat everyone with respect
(even the person whose head you're trying to smash in).

...keep your promises.
...show self-control.
...treat important enemies well
if you capture them.

As if all that isn't enough, you'll find priests constantly telling you what to do. Priests have all sorts of rules, but most knights take these with a pinch of salt.

So, remember, knights need to be...

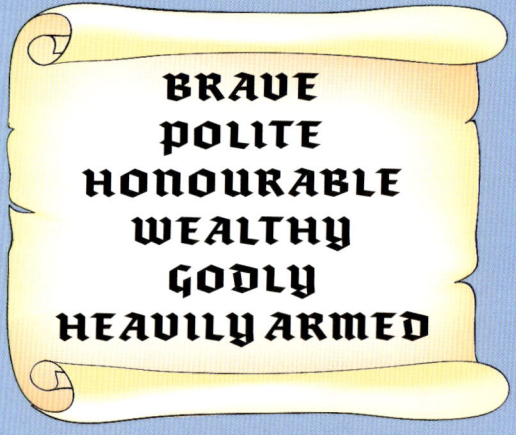

**BRAVE
POLITE
HONOURABLE
WEALTHY
GODLY
HEAVILY ARMED**

Still think you're up to it?

Try these questions to discover if you're made of the **Knight Stuff**...

1. Your army is about to take part in a **crucial battle**. You want to help out, but you can't see very well. Do you...

a) **Stand well back** and shout, "GO ON, LADS!!!" as loudly as you can?

b) **Borrow a bow** and fire arrows in every direction?

c) Tie your horse between two other knights' horses, grab a sword and **charge into battle?**

Let me at them!

2. Your **helmet is badly bent** when an enemy wallops you with his sword. After the battle, you can't take the helmet off. Do you...

a) Decide to wear it for the **rest of your life**?

b) **Go on a diet** until you're thin enough to take it off?

Hold still... this'll only take a moment.

c) Ask a **friendly blacksmith to hammer your head** until the helmet is back in shape?

If you answered **c)** to both questions, you might just make a knight yet. These are the options that famous knights – King John of Bohemia (who couldn't see), and William Marshal – took when they found themselves in such tricky situations.

Sadly, John of Bohemia died on the battlefield. William Marshal just had a sore head.

But there is one final (and, frankly, bizarre) part of chivalry you'll need to get to grips with. It's coming up on the next page...

Courtly love

Knights are expected to dedicate all their honourable deeds to a particular lady. Here's how it works...

First, **choose a lady** – preferably a wealthy and important one (a queen if you're feeling ambitious). It doesn't matter if she's already married, and you don't even need to have met her.

Next, decide that you **love your lady more than anyone else in the whole wide world**, and that you'd do absolutely anything to prove it.

WARNING: you may have to give up sleeping and eating to show how truly besotted you are… and that's only the start. (I did say it was bizarre.)

Your lady may never actually talk to you – or she might call you rude names if she does – but don't let this dim your passion. You'll just have to **bite your tongue and keep smiling.** Remember, in the world of courtly love, it simply shows how much better than you she is.

It might take you a while to get the hang of courtly love, so try another quick question:

You are **Sir Lancelot, GKOAT** (the Greatest Knight of All Time), and you're head over heels in love with Queen Guinevere. You're taking part in a contest against other knights and Guinevere asks you to lose on purpose. Do you...

a) **Try to change her mind** by brilliantly beating all the other knights?

b) Meekly obey her order, and **let everyone else thrash you?**

c) **Throw a tantrum and sulk** in the corner, refusing to take part?

As any knight worth his salt would have done, Lancelot chose **b)**. He adored Guinevere so much that he didn't mind making himself look a complete nincompoop for her. That's crazy – I mean, *courtly* – love for you.

Where you fit in

Before you start your training, you should know where you fit in. In the **medieval world** (especially during 'knight' time, c. 1000–1500), all knights are **not** equal.

There are three types:

King
(top knight; leads a country's army)

Noble
(posh knight who owns loads of land and fights for his king)

Average knight
(who fights for a noble)
This is YOU!

Protecting peasants

Peasants

As an **average knight**, you'll fight in your **noble's army**, and in return he'll give you some of his land to live on.

There'll be lots of **peasants** living on your new land, and it's part of your job to **protect them** from enemy soldiers, marauding madmen and over-enthusiastic salesmen.

Military service

One more thing: you'll be expected to fight for your noble for **40 days a year.** Don't book your holidays yet though. If wars drag on longer than expected (and they usually do), you'll be fighting to the bitter end. (But you do at least get paid for the extra days you fight.)

Can I go home now?

If there's no discouraging you, it's time you started your training. Good luck – but don't say you weren't warned...

Chapter Two
Knight school

A budding knight should **start training** at the age of **six or seven**. If you're older than that already, just try not to look too tall. Training begins when you're **sent away from home** all on your own to live in a castle with a lord who's already a knight. You'd better get packed.

Starting out
A lowly page

Unless you come from a very rich family, you'll start out at the bottom. You'll be known as a **page** – yup, you're now a **servant**. Even the other servants will order you about, and you'll find yourself cleaning armour, serving meals and doing all the jobs that no one else wants.

Clean that lot, would you?

And that's it for the next few years. Your best bet is to keep your head down and try to stay out of trouble.

A higher squire

Once you're a teenager, as long as you've stayed on the right side of your lord, you become a **squire**. Now things get more interesting...

 You look after your lord's horses.

 You clean and polish his sword. (Watch out for the sharp end.)

 You help your lord put on his armour. With dozens of separate pieces and fiddly straps, this can take as long as an hour.

Exciting fighting

As a squire, you also finally get your hands on some weapons and armour of your own. If you can actually pick them up, that is. You'll find they're a **lot heavier** than you might expect...

So you'd better make sure you're as **strong as an ox.** Try running around the castle grounds in a suit of armour – or, failing that, a barrel.

Once you've got arms and legs of steel, it's time for some weapons training.

If you can't find heavy armour to run in, use whatever you can find.

Prance with a lance

First up, there's the **lance**. It may only look like a **long wooden pole with a metal spike** on the end, but it's the reason why knights are the **most feared warriors** in the world.

Your lance will be more than twice as tall as you.

Tuck the blunt end under your right arm and press the lance tightly against your body.

Hold the lance with your right hand, and try to keep it nice and steady.

Your lance has a guard, called a vamplate, to protect your hand.

37

Once you've got the hang of that, try aiming your lance at a **target** while riding a horse. It won't be easy, since its length – 3m (10ft) – means the lance will probably wobble. Worse still, miss the target and you'll get whacked on the back of the head.

Target, called a quintain

Ouch!

Horsing around

Of course, it's no use being a wizard with a lance if you can't **control your horse**.

The tips on the next page should help.

Spur

While you're training, you'll be given **spurs** (pieces of spiky metal) to wear on your ankles.

To spur on the horse and make it go faster, press the spikes into its sides – but not too hard!

If you want the horse to **turn**, pull the reins **gently** to one side...

...and, to make an **emergency stop**, pull back **sharply** on the reins.

Aaagh!

Sword play

Your other main weapon is, of course, your **trusty sword**.

Now you're talking!

The most popular sword is called a "**hand-and-a-half**" sword. Although you *can* hold it with your right hand, while holding a shield in your left...

...the handle is long enough for you to grip it with both hands, for those extra powerful blows.

Being courteous

Apart from learning to fight, you also need to learn the finer things in life, such as:

 How to dance elegantly. (Remember to dress appropriately.)

 How to treat a lady.

Oops... Pardon.

 How to eat politely. (Using your fingers is OK, but never burp or spit.)

Tonight's the knight

By the time you're 20, you should be an **unstoppable fighting machine** with beautiful manners, which means you're ready to become a knight.

This is a HUGE moment in a squire's life. You'd think there would be a party. Instead, for the sons of wealthy, powerful nobles, there's a slightly weird ceremony.

Getting ready

First, your fellow squires will give you a **cold bath**.

Next, dressed in a smart tunic and cloak, you have to spend an **entire night kneeling in a church**, praying that you'll be a good knight.

No nodding off, now...

Being dubbed

In the morning, you kneel in front of the person who's going to make you a knight. Only another knight, or a queen, can do this.

The knight touches you on the shoulder with his sword. This is called **dubbing**. Stay still – that sword is SHARP.

Then take a deep breath because – woo hoo! – you're a **knight**. You've made it! Give yourself a pat on the back.

Double-quick dubbing

Priests think all knights should be created this way, because they want knights to fight for the Church. But don't worry if your dad's not rich enough for you to take part in a fancy ceremony – most squires get made into knights in two minutes on the **battlefield**.

Quick, they're coming!

You'd better be ready to kneel at short notice.

Presents!

If you become a knight through the ceremony route, you'll be presented with a sword, shield and pair of spurs of your own. These show the world that you're a knight – so try not to lose them.

Now where did I put those spurs?

All knights are addressed as "Sir", so if your name is Ramsbottom you're now Sir Ramsbottom – how about that?

Kitting yourself out

Now you're a knight, you'll need lots more equipment. Your lance and sword will be your main weapons, but there are plenty of others you could use.

You need to know about all the weapons at your disposal. After all, your enemies are sure to be using them too.

The only thing to fear is fear itself – oh, and the spiky metal objects your enemy will throw at you.

Wicked weapons

First up: **a dagger** for close combat. Just force it through a gap in your enemy's armour. (Ouch!)

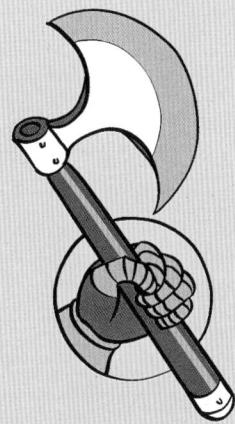

A battle axe: bash your enemies at close range, or hurl it from a distance.

A pollaxe is useful if you find yourself on foot during a battle. When enemy knights charge at you, give it a good swing and bring them crashing down.

Maces are short sticks with heavy metal ends. One hard thwack with one of these can crush an enemy's armour.

Flails are like maces, but worse. They have spiky iron balls attached to the end. Try not to be hit by one – it will crush your armour and shatter your bones to smithereens.

Armour-plated

With all those vicious weapons being whirled around, you need all the armour you can get – and fortunately there's plenty of it.

In the really old days, knights wore **mail** armour, made from thousands of tiny iron rings linked together.

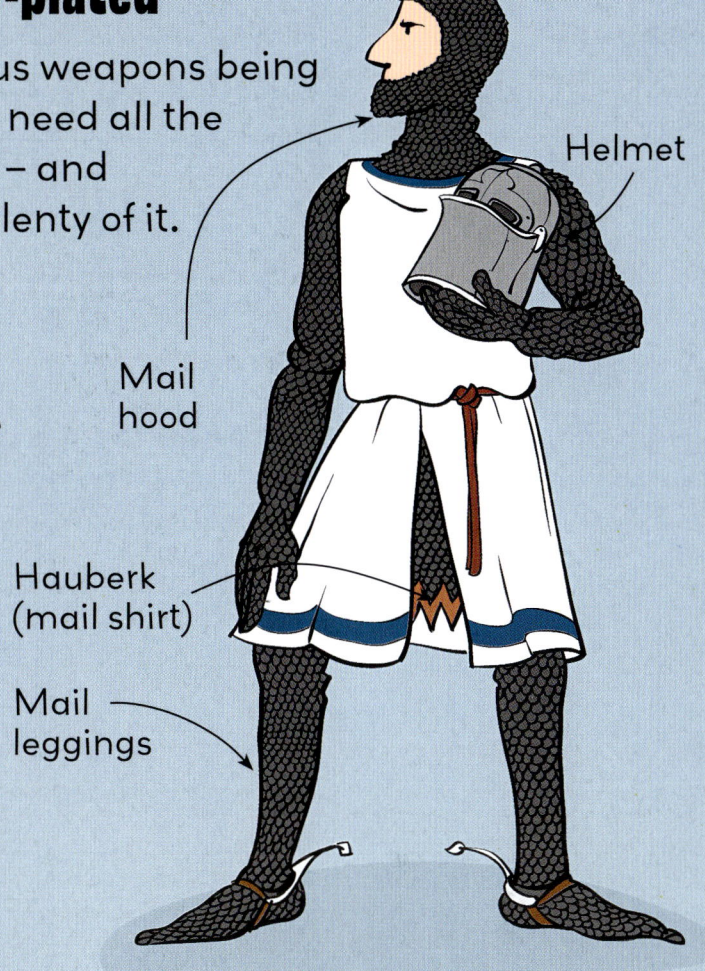

Helmet

Mail hood

Hauberk (mail shirt)

Mail leggings

Mail offers some protection, but a well-aimed arrow will give you a nasty stomach ache.

And all those iron rings are heavy: imagine having to fight while giving a friend a piggyback and you'll get an idea of how it feels.

49

The latest fashion for the really rich knight is far more fancy – a suit of plate armour.

Those sheets of metal may look heavy (and they are, VERY heavy), but this outfit is surprisingly flexible. It's tough too, giving you more chance against pesky archers.

Each sheet is designed to cover up as much as possible.

Suits have hinges and joints for flexibility, as seen here on the foot – so flexible you can even bend your toes.

Stay cool

A word of warning: things can get **very sweaty** inside plate armour.

Don't go running around unless you absolutely have to.

Coats of arms

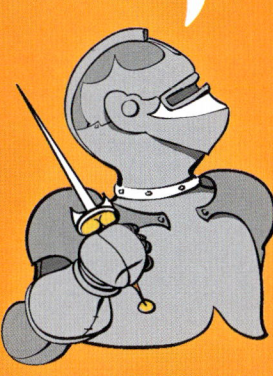

"It's me!"

"Who?"

When a knight's wearing a helmet, it can be hard to see who he is. This is awkward in battle, when it helps to know who your friends are and who's trying to slice you into tiny pieces.

That's why you need a **coat of arms**: a pattern or picture on your shield, to show who you are. No two knights are allowed to have the same coat of arms, so don't go copying someone else's.

"How dare you, sir! This is MINE!"

For a look at what design your shield might have, see page 117.

Clubs for knights

Another good idea at this point is to join an **order** – a group of knights who hang around together, protect each other and go to the same parties. The world is a dangerous place, so it's good to have friends.

Each order has its own symbol. There's the Order of the Garter, the Order of the Golden Fleece – even the Order of the Elephant.

A squire of your own

Now that you're a knight, you also get your **very own squire** to look after your horses and help you put your armour on. Take care of the lad.

This squire is feeling nervous – it's his first day.

Horses for courses

You're nearly ready now – all that's left is to pop down to the stables and buy yourself some horses. You'll need three types:

Destrier (Mad-Eyed Monster): an enormous, powerful war horse. Try not to annoy it.

Courser (Speed Demon): runs like the wind, so perfect for sending messages. Keep an eye on it.

Palfrey (Humble Trotter): not strong or fast, but super comfortable. Your bottom will thank you for riding a palfrey.

Chapter Three
To battle!

It's the moment you've been waiting for: time to get your armour dirty with some **proper fighting**. If your noble isn't fighting any battles just now, try your luck abroad.

Battle tactics

The thing to remember on the battlefield is that you and your fellow knights will only win if you **work together**. The classic battle tactic is the **cavalry charge**, and it goes like this...

1. Get together with some other knights and raise your lances menacingly. Try to look fierce.

2. When you get the signal, gallop at the enemy as fast as you can, holding your lance firmly in front of you.

If everything goes according to plan, most of your enemies will be impaled. You'll find they won't give you much trouble after that.

On the battlefield

As a **charging knight**, you'll be the **most feared force** on the battlefield. Even when you're vastly outnumbered by enemy foot soldiers, if you get your charge right, victory should be yours in the blink of an eye.

Knights charge in small groups.

A standard bearer shows the coat of arms of the lord who's commanding the army.

Beware being cut off from your army.

Some foot soldiers stick out their pikes to give you a prickly welcome.

Enemy tactics

In a perfect battle, it's smash, bang, wallop and you've won. But recently foot soldiers have been developing some nasty tricks to stop you in your tracks. Here are a few of the more devious ones to look out for...

Savage stakes

Sharp wooden stakes are hammered into the ground and tilted in your direction, so you can't charge at your enemies. (Well, you *can*, but it might be rather squelchy and painful.)

Perilous potholes

This is an equally irritating trick. When you're charging at full speed with your lance aimed at someone's head, the last thing you want is for your horse to trip. Your enemies know this, of course, so they dig lots of holes on the battlefield.

Annoying archers

These are your deadliest enemies of all – canny characters you'll soon learn to look out for.

They stay well back so you can't reach them with your lance, and then send dozens of arrows whistling through the air at you.

The cheek of it!

Expert archers can **fire an arrow every three seconds.**

Ransoms

If you're unlucky enough to fall into enemy hands, don't panic – your enemies are unlikely to kill you, because they can make very good money selling you back to your own side. (If you're wealthy, that is – penniless foot soldiers end up dead.)

Castle warfare

There are loads of ways to **attack** a castle. First, **lay siege** to it (surround it with your army). Then try these tricks...

SIEGE TOWERS: Wheel them close, and charge!

BATTERING RAMS: Huge logs inside wooden huts. Swing the log back and forth to smash the castle door.

SCALING LADDERS: Just climb up and in – but watch out for those enemy archers.

LOW-DOWN and DIRTY: Sneak your way in through the toilet waste pipe. Ugh!

TREBUCHETS: Giant catapults that hurl rocks more than 300m (1,000ft). If you're in a bad mood, hurl dead animals to spread disease in the castle.

COLLAPSE THE CASTLE: Dig a tunnel, then start a fire in it. The tunnel will cave in (and so, with any luck, will the castle).

Starve them out

If you don't fancy attacking a castle, the oldest trick in the book is to **do absolutely nothing** at all. Just surround it, and then stand there playing hide and seek until the army inside runs out of food.

If you're easily bored, you'll find **poisoning** the castle's water supply will speed things up a bit.

Fighting back

You're just as likely to find yourself **defending** a castle as attacking one, so you'll be pleased to learn that there are plenty of ways to keep the hordes from swarming in.

Throwing things

Arrows · Boiling water · Red-hot sand · Desperate measures

One effective ploy is to pelt the brutes below you with anything that comes to hand. Castle walls have handy gaps for just this purpose.

The cruel crow

Another popular **counter-siege** weapon is the **crow** – a pole with a hook on the end. Simply lower it over the castle wall like a giant fishing rod...

...scoop an enemy of your choice high into the air...

...and then drop him back to earth with a bump. That's one down!

Fires and ditches

Push **siege towers** away with long sticks, and pepper them with flaming arrows to set fire to them. You can also creep out at night and **dig ditches** near the castle, to topple the towers.

The water test

To check for **enemy tunnels**, place **bowls of water** in different places around the castle. If the water ripples, you know some scoundrel is digging beneath it. Simply dig your own tunnel to meet theirs, then burst through and pummel the tunnellers.

Crazy crusades

One popular way to find a good battle is to join a crusade. A crusade is a huge campaign against non-Christian people in other lands, organized by the Church. This is your chance to go off on an adventure. You'll get to see the world and, with luck, you can prove how brave you are.

Officially, the idea is to protect Christians overseas and even try to persuade other people to convert to Christianity. But actually most crusades are simply a chance to **grab fortune** and **glory**.

Off to the east

The biggest crusades head for the **Holy Land** in the Middle East, to try to capture the city of Jerusalem from its Muslim rulers. But Jerusalem is a holy city for Muslims as well, so the locals are quite eager to hang onto it.

In the future, people will probably think these Crusades were a **TERRIBLE idea** – and any Crusader victories will probably be short-lived – but it's where the fighting is for a knight.

On the plus side, they are bringing some benefits. You could return with:

 Great ideas for new castle designs

 Spices and silks

 Amazing skills in map-making, especially if you find your way home.

If you do head that way, you may well encounter brilliant Muslim archers, who fight on horseback.

You've got company

Hold on, there – you can't just set off. The preparation needed before you go is mind-boggling. You'll have to organize supplies (food, drink and clean socks), and back-up. For a start, you'll need a friendly armourer to join you – or what will you do when your armour needs fixing mid-battle?

At least you won't be lonely. Thousands of people are bound to join you on the way, in search of treasure, land and a shortcut to heaven.

Holy knights

If you get into a sticky situation out in the Holy Land, you might find that a mysterious band of knights whizzes over the horizon and saves you, just in the nick of time.

These are the **Knights Templar**: warrior monks from Europe who've formed an order dedicated to protecting Christians.

Tempted by the Templars?

You might like to join the Templars, but you'll have to take lots of religious vows. You won't be able to spend your time falling for ladies and playing cards like all those other knights.

Templars promise to live a life of poverty, but actually they're rich as kings. They've even set up newfangled businesses called **banks** – but who knows if these will ever catch on.

Helpful Hospitallers

The other major religious order in the East is called the **Knights Hospitaller.** As you may have guessed, they spend their time offering hospitality, and looking after sick, poor or injured Christians in hospitals they've built.

You'd think Hospitallers and Templars would be the best of friends but, as it happens, they loathe each other.

If you spot two knights brawling in the street, the chances are that one is a Templar and the other a Hospitaller.

Crusader castles

The Templars and Hospitallers have built themselves lots of huge castles in the Holy Land. If you're on the run with a few hundred angry enemies in hot pursuit, head for one of these.

Chapter Four
Home for the knight

When you've fought a few wars and made pots of money, it's time to settle down and admire your bruises in a **castle of your own**, instead of trying to demolish someone else's. You might be lucky enough to inherit a castle, but if not, you'll have to steal or build one.

Castle browsing

There are several different homes available to the wealthy knight looking for his first castle…

Marvellous motte and bailey

This charming residence is an example of an early type of castle: a quaint **wooden tower** on a **hilltop** (the motte) with an **enclosed yard** below it (the bailey). When an angry army or your mad uncle Geoffrey turns up, everyone dashes up the hill and hides in the tower.

Bridge with small drawbridges top and bottom – raise these to keep people out.

Stables

Great Hall

Wooden fence, or palisade

Earth mound and ditch

Chapel

There's just one drawback – all that wood. If anyone starts a fire, the place will burn down faster than you can say,

"Please don't knock that candle over."

Solid stone tower

Next is a more secure castle. The walls are made of **stone**, so the fire risk is smaller and it's harder for people to bash their way in.

Extra protection comes in the form of a wide ditch, known as the **moat**. (The one shown here has been filled with water, which should make you even safer.)

This place is more expensive than the motte and bailey, but you'll certainly sleep more soundly behind all those solid walls.

Visitors have to wait to be let across the drawbridge.

The moat is ideal for skimming stones.

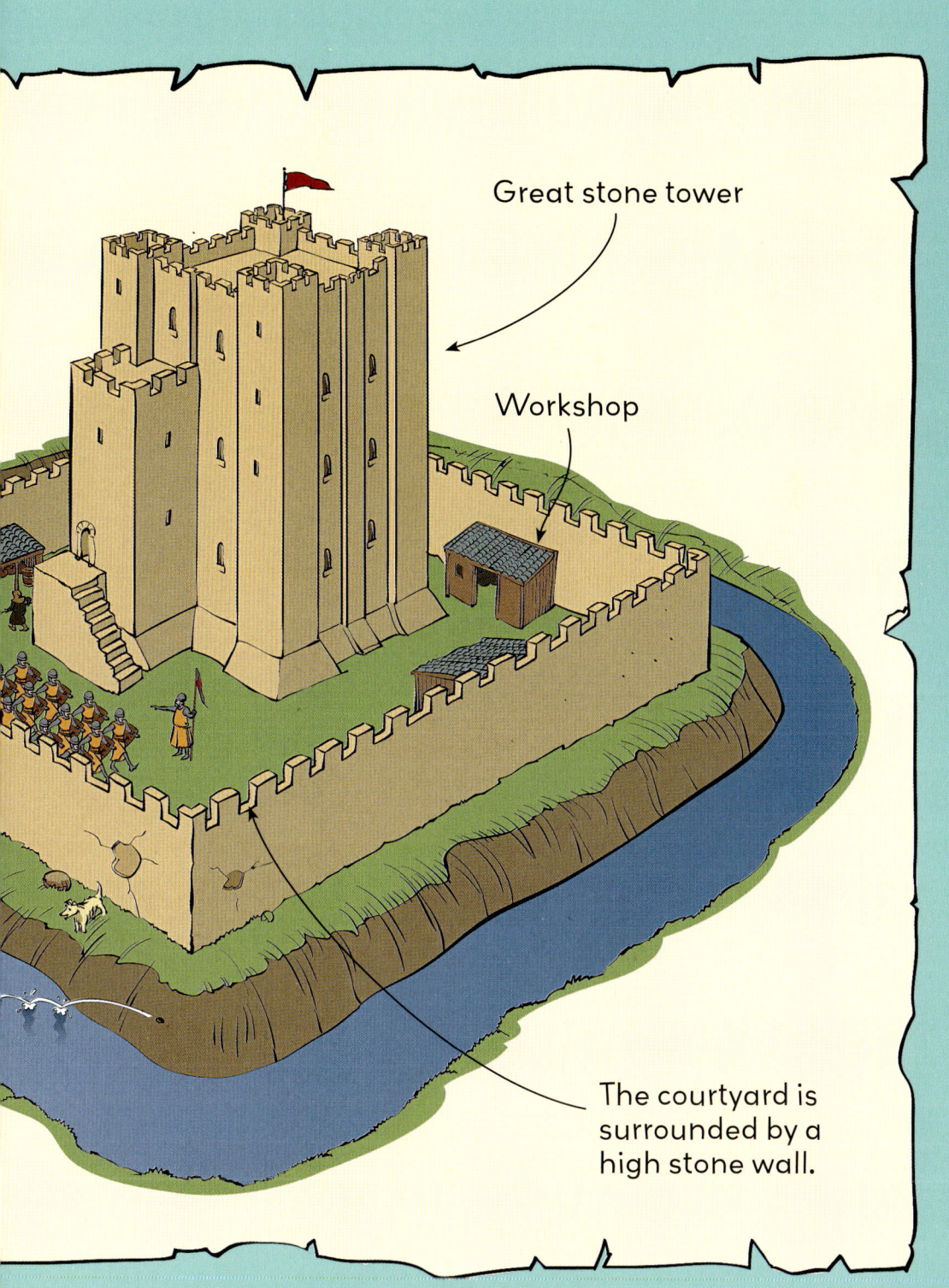

Cunning concentric castle

Ta-da! Here's the latest thing in castle design. Invaders are kept out by a **series of walls**, one inside another.

This castle will cost you a fortune, but it's so safe that it comes with a **one-year non-invadable guarantee.**

If you want to stop the neighbours from popping round unexpectedly to chop off your head, it's the best that money can buy.

The outer walls are lower than the inner walls.

Approaching enemies

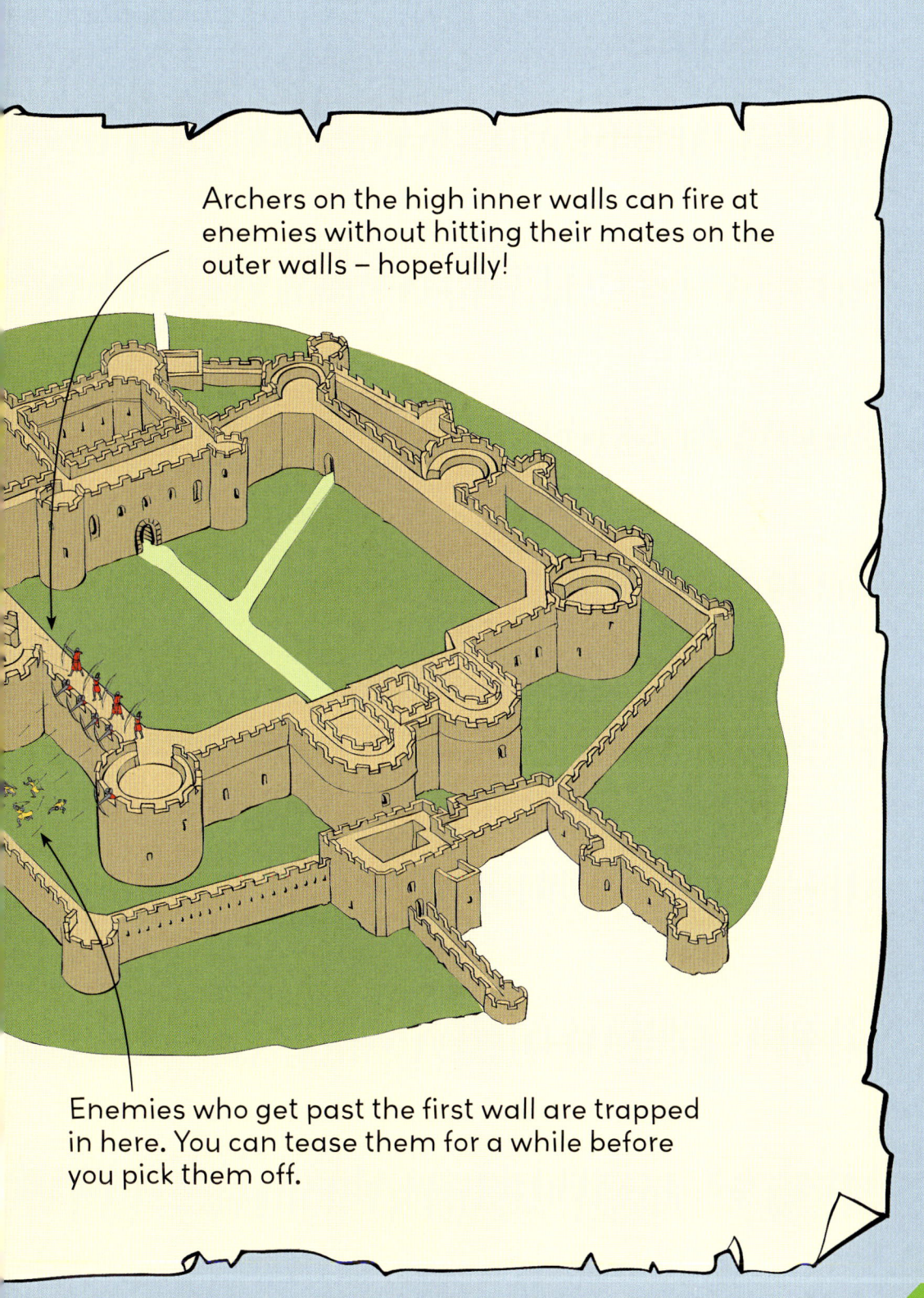

Archers on the high inner walls can fire at enemies without hitting their mates on the outer walls – hopefully!

Enemies who get past the first wall are trapped in here. You can tease them for a while before you pick them off.

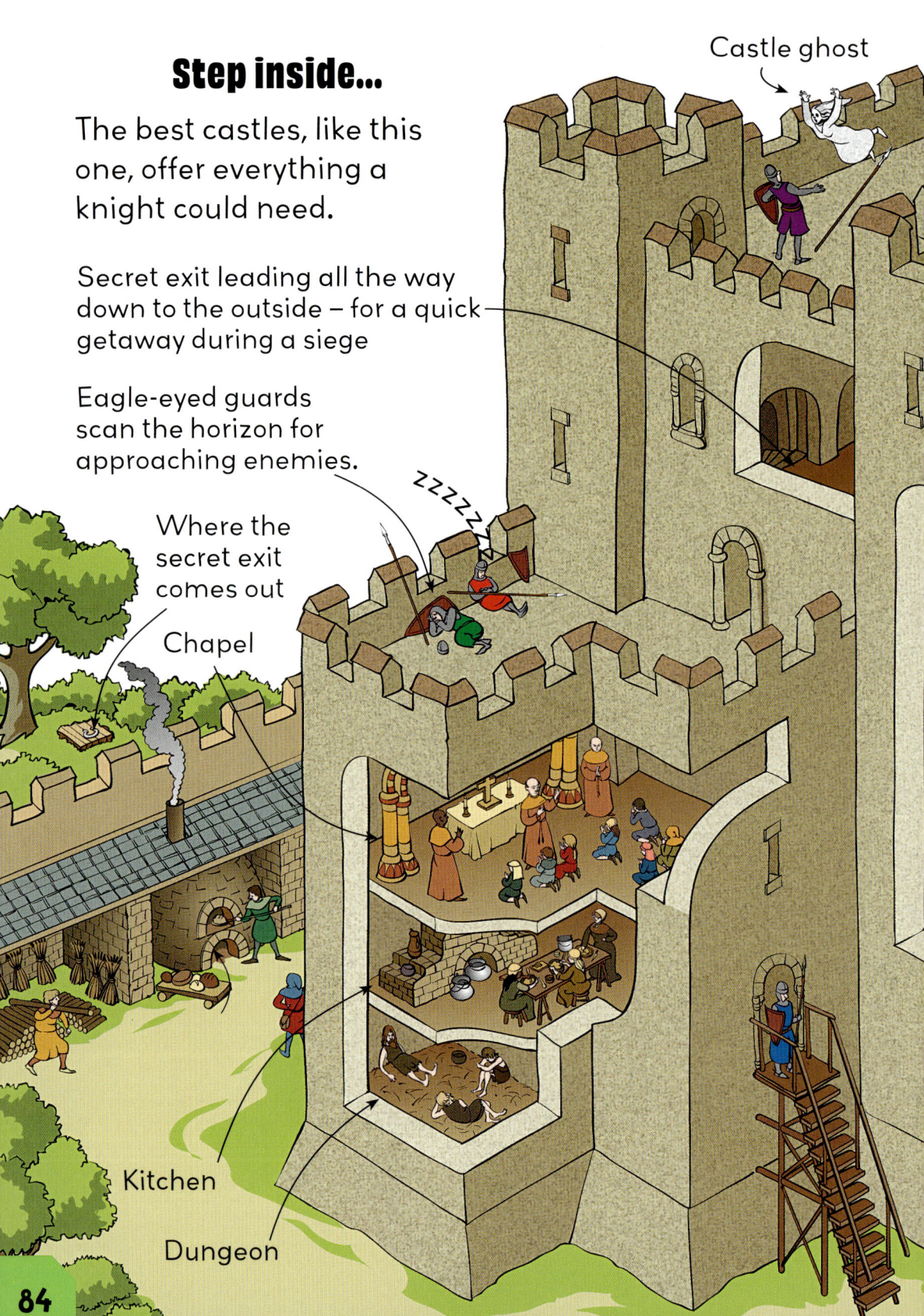

Castle life

Whichever castle you go for, you'll need to be prepared for a few hardships. Even for the wealthiest knight, life isn't exactly luxurious.

Castle hassles

I wish someone would start a war. At least fighting keeps you warm.

Whistling wind: Castles are **breezy.** A few of the latest ones do have some glass, at least in the chapel. Others have shutters or simply bits of oiled cloth stuck up to keep out the draughts.

Even so, bring lots of warm clothes when you move in.

Toilet trouble: The only toilet is a hole, called a garderobe.

Anything that goes in there whizzes straight down a chute – either into the inner courtyard, or the moat.

Frozen food: Because of the fire risk, the kitchen is separate from the rooms where you live – and eat.

The downside is that your food has plenty of time to go cold during its long journey to your table.

Castle perks

But it's not all gloom and doom – there are **fun things** about castle life too, such as:

Your own personal jester! His job is to make you laugh and keep you entertained, whether you feel in the mood for a joke, a song, acrobatics or juggling. (And if all that fails to lift your spirits, try having him thrown in the moat.)

A spooky dungeon for prisoners?

If your castle doesn't have a dungeon, you can always use a forgotten, unpleasant corner to house people who owe you money or are trying to take over your land.

A food-taster:

This lucky man gets to nibble all your food before you touch it, just to make sure it tastes OK – and that it's not poisoned.

Bounteous banquets

Every lord loves a good **feast** in his castle. But it's not just about eating – it's a way to display your wealth and show people exactly what you think of them. Where guests are seated shows just how important they are.

The lord and lady sit in the middle of this high table.

The most important guests sit around the lord.

The next most important people

Castle capers

A few ways to pass the time between wars are **card games**, **board games**, **chess** and **dice**. Another favourite knightly hobby is merrelles, a fancy version of **noughts and crosses**.

You might also like to try a spot of **hunting** in the forest – the most popular hobby for knights. (It's less popular with animals.) Your chef will happily make use of most things you kill (unless it's a fox), but knights hunt for fun too.

The less important (but still slightly important) people

Musicians entertain the guests from a gallery.

The lowest of the low

Chapter Five
Tournaments and challenges

In between battles you'll need to keep your skills sharp, and this is where **tournaments** come in: a whole lot of knights getting together on a big field to practise fighting.

It's supposed to be a friendly fight but it doesn't always turn out like that, and if a knight gets carried away he can end up with a dead body on the end of his lance. So keep your wits about you.

Tournaments are also one of the best ways to **find fame.** There'll be plenty of spectators watching from the safety of their seats, so this is your big chance to let the world know what a spectacularly fine warrior you are, and to show off your very best armour.

Muddy mêlées

The simplest game at a tournament is a **mêlée** (say "mellay"). Well, perhaps "game" isn't quite the right word. It's basically a battle, and a savage, bloody one at that. All the knights split into two teams, each led by a lord, and then beat each other up.

Except for generally trying to break people's bones, the aim is to **capture as many knights from the other team** as possible. Then you force your prisoners to pay a ransom. If they can't pay, you take their horses and armour.

Rules?

There are almost **no rules**.

You can **use any weapon** you like...

THONK!

...you can **gang up** on a single knight from the other team...

...you can even pull silly faces and then pounce on your opponent while he's laughing.

The only thing you can't do is try to kill another knight. But you might well kill someone by mistake, and no one is likely to mind too much if you do.

A safe area – if you're in trouble, leap into one, and no one can touch you until you step outside it.

Muted mêlées

Those peace-loving priests keep trying to ban mêlées altogether and some knights do prefer to fight with **wooden swords**, to keep the deaths and maimings to a minimum.

But you can still find a good old-fashioned scrap with real weapons and plenty of blood if you look hard enough.

Bone-jangling jousts

This is the main event: dramatic and dangerous. A **joust** involves only **two knights**. Everyone else will be watching, so try not to make a fool of yourself.

Try to catch the eye at a joust with your unusual headgear.

In early jousts, knights sat on their horses holding a lance, and then galloped towards each other. The idea was to send the other knight flying.

Hey – no one said anything about him having a lance as well!

But the number of cracked skulls and broken legs means that these days there's a (slightly) safer version...

Safety first

Knights are now separated by a barrier called a **tilt**. You charge along opposite sides of the tilt, which means you **can't collide** head-on.

And the **goal** isn't to knock the other knight over, just **to break the tip of your lance** against him. If you manage this, it shows you've struck him fair and square.

I'm doing it all for you, Griselda, my darling!

You use lances with blunt ends, so you can't accidentally skewer each other.

You might like to wear a lady's scarf or veil while jousting, to show how much you adore her.

Single combat

If you're defeated in a joust, you can leap off your horse and **fight** your opponent **on foot**. But be warned: the exact number of blows to be struck is agreed before the combat starts. You thump the other knight, while he defends. Then, of course, it's his turn to thump you.

There's no horse to escape on here – it's just you and the other knight.

Handy heralds

There'll be hundreds of you gathered at a big tournament and you'll each have your own **coat of arms.** So to help the spectators follow the action, there are handy men called heralds.

Only another 5,048 to learn...

Heralds train for years so they can recognize every single coat of arms. They announce the names of all the knights taking part, and then they referee the contests.

Heralds for hire

If you can afford it, hire a **personal herald**. Before each contest, he'll go on and on about how many battles you've won and what a demon you are with a lance. (This is great, but it does put pressure on. Everyone will snigger if you fall off your horse after thirty seconds.)

A tournament in full swing

The host of the tournament and his family have the best seats in the house.

Winner's cup

The champion jouster struts his stuff.

This defeated knight has lost his horse, his sword *and* his spurs.

Heralds in peril

You'll also see **heralds at battles**. They note the name of any knight who's being cowardly.

Oh dear, Sir Shudderwimp is crying again...

(As if fighting for your life wasn't enough, you get marked out of ten while you're at it.)

Before they fight, knights can tell a herald their last requests – which brings us to the **grisly part** of a herald's job...

After the action, heralds must walk around the battlefield making a note of all the dead knights – or pieces of dead knights – they see.

Pas d'armes

Failed to make a name for yourself at a tournament? Try **re-enacting a scene** from an old tale of heroism, taking the starring role. This is a pas d'armes (say "pa-darm"). It might sound theatrical – but the fighting is very real.

You could grab your sword and stand under an oak tree. Then let it be known that you're staying put for a whole year and you'll take on anyone who fancies it.

Now, when I said "anyone"...

This is a chivalrous way of saying, "Come and have a go if you think you're hard enough." But it also proves that you're just as heroic as the legendary knights of the past. (Unless you get beaten to a pulp by a passing little old lady.)

Chapter Six
Knight notes

To give you some final inspiration, here are a few of the **most famous knights** of all time. One day, if you become a truly exceptional knight, you might stand alongside them in the chivalric **Hall of Fame**.

(The first three probably never existed, but so many knights are inspired by stories about them that most people think of them as real.)

Knights to remember

King Arthur

The **most legendary knight** of all, and an example to everyone. No one is sure when or where he lived (though he may be based on memories of a real chief, almost certainly **not** named Arthur). According to some stories, his court was at a place called **Camelot** and he led an order of warriors who gathered at a round table.

The **Knights of the Round Table** spent most of their lives obsessively searching for the Holy Grail, a sacred cup from which Jesus Christ is supposed to have drunk at the Last Supper.

Sir Lancelot

The **bravest and most brilliant** of Arthur's knights, Lancelot is famous as one of the greatest warriors of all time.

Apparently, he once crawled along a bridge made from the razor-sharp blade of a giant sword in order to rescue a queen – not bad, eh?

Sir Galahad

Lancelot's son, Galahad, was the most perfect, pure and chivalrous knight of the lot – even taking the **GKOAT** crown from his dad.

When he arrived at Camelot, he was seated at the **Siege Perilous** – a chair at the Round Table reserved for the greatest knight of all, and fatal to anyone else.

Galahad's finest hour came when he found the elusive Holy Grail. But then he lost it again – doh!

Rodrigo de Vivar (El Cid)

A legendary **Spanish knight** who fought in the crusades in Spain – for the Muslims as well as the Christians.

Whichever side he was on, **he always won**, and when he died in 1099 he had never lost a battle. The other knights nicknamed him **El Cid** – the Lord.

William Marshal

One of the most brilliant knights of his time, Marshal was a **star at tournaments.**

Mind you, he wasn't above the odd dirty trick — one of his favourite ruses was to grab the bridle of another knight's horse, then gallop off into the distance, dragging the unfortunate fellow and his horse with him.

Then wily William would force his startled prisoner to pay a huge ransom before he let him go. Some people have a strange idea of chivalry.

Prince Edward (the Black Prince)

An English knight who was an **amazing commander** in battle.

He led his army to victory at the **Battle of Poitiers** despite the fact that his enemies had more than twice as many knights as him. He *may* have got his nickname from his dastardly deeds.

Marshal Boucicaut

This **French knight** was already a fearsome fighter at 16. Famously nimble, he could leap onto his horse while wearing full armour.

He once told his army's watchmen he'd cut off their ears if they upset the other knights by warning them the enemy was near. (His army was ambushed and slaughtered.)

Your own coat of arms

Finally, in case you fancy having your own **coat of arms**, there are some ideas on the next few pages. But don't forget to get the **king's approval** – it's usually his herald who designs them.

A coat of arms isn't literally a coat, but you can still wear one with aplomb – and so can your horse.

The first thing to do is choose a style. Basic designs, like these, are known as **ordinaries**:

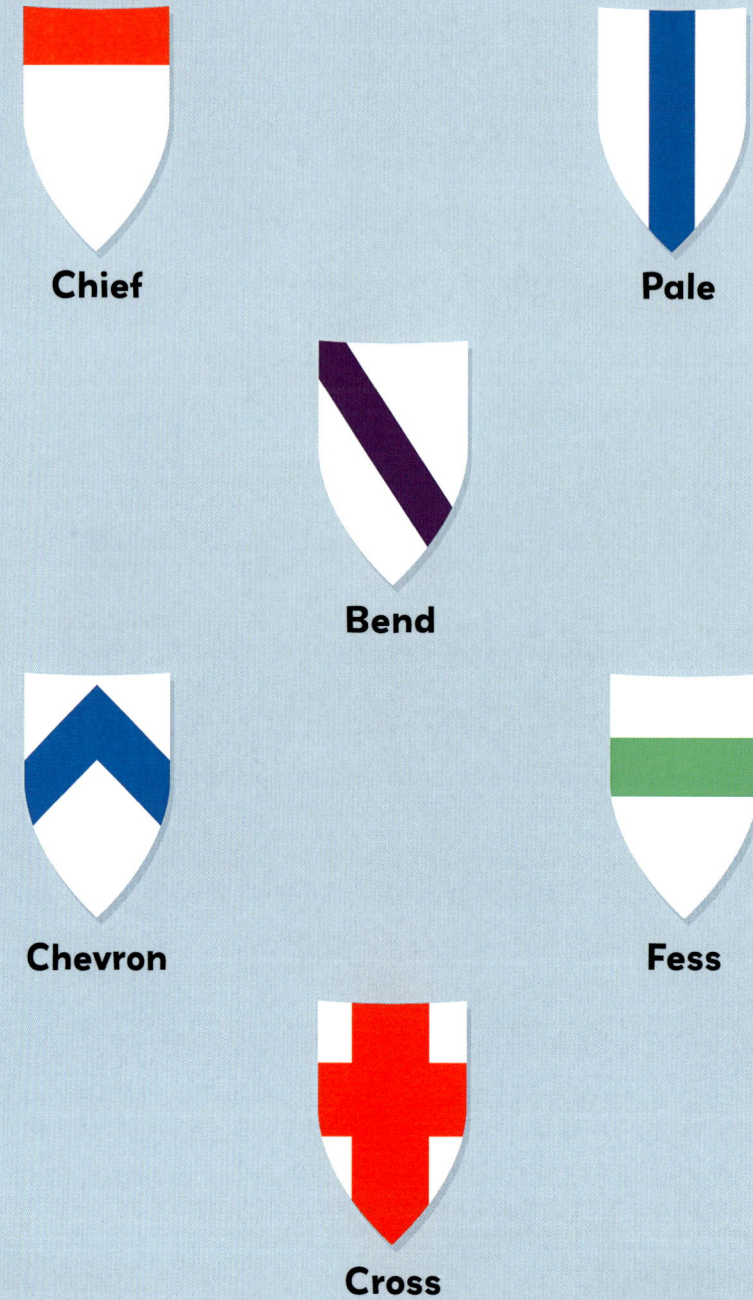

Chief

Pale

Bend

Chevron

Fess

Cross

Pile　　　　　　　　**Saltire**

Then there are **partitions**:

Per pale　　　　　　**Per bend**

Per fess

Quarterly　　　　　　**Per chevron**

Then they get LESS ordinary:

You can even put a picture on your shield. Animals, monsters, fish, weapons, flowers – all feature on coats of arms. Here are a few you might consider:

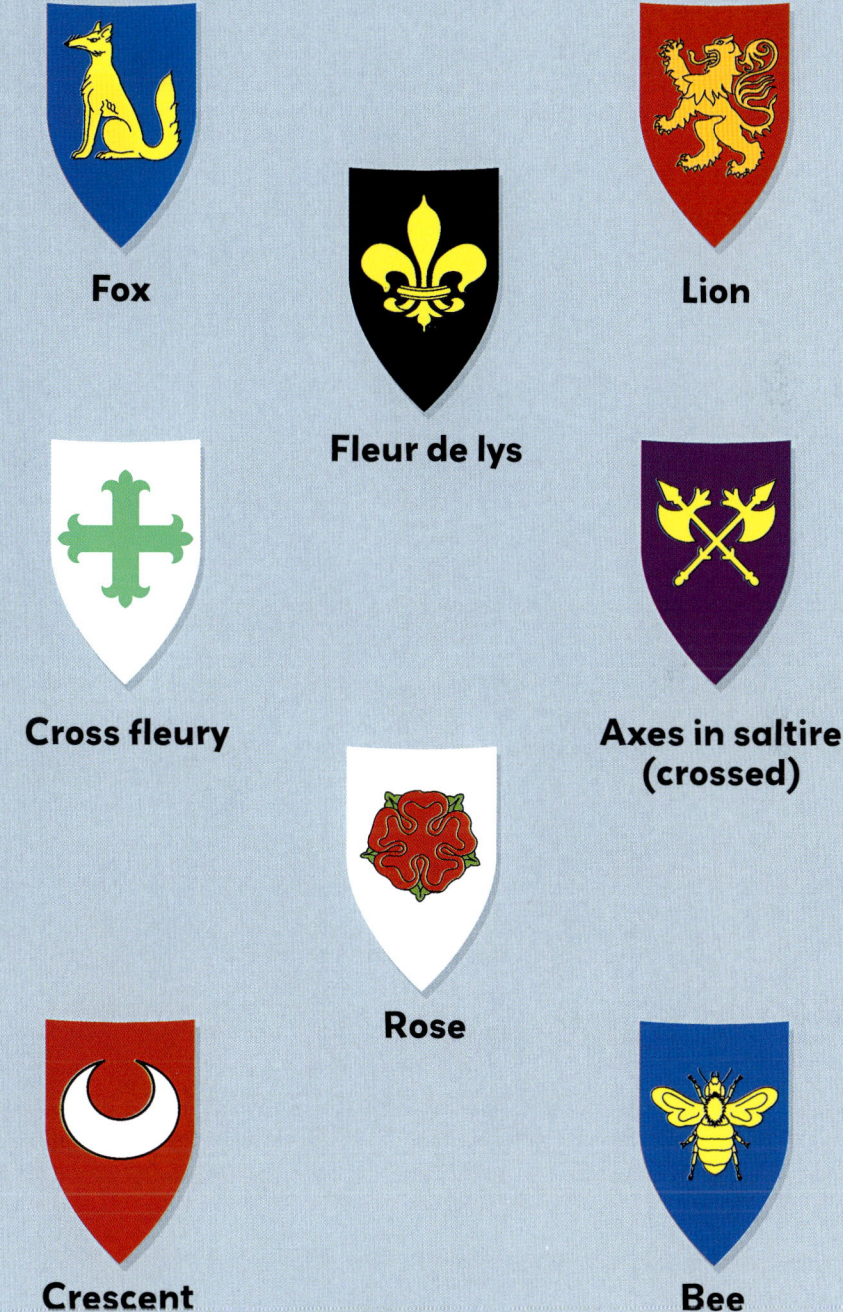

Fox

Fleur de lys

Lion

Cross fleury

Axes in saltire (crossed)

Rose

Crescent

Bee

Lots of knights have a picture which suggests what their name is. So if you're Sir Appleby, your shield might look like this:

If you're Sir Eagleton, you might consider this:

And if you're called Bottomley... well, you get the idea.

Usborne Quicklinks

For links to websites where you can find out more about knights, coats of arms, and how to defend a castle, go to **usborne.com/Quicklinks** and type in the title of this book.

Usborne Publishing is not responsible for the content of external websites. Children should be supervised online. Please follow the online safety guidelines at usborne.com/Quicklinks

Index

archers 50, 62, 72, 83
armour 10, 13, 35, 49, 50, 53, 73, 116
    mail armour 49
    plate armour 50
Arthur, King 110
axes 47

banks 75
banquets 90-91
baths 42
battles 21, 44, 58-59
    enemies 60, 61, 62, 63
    potholes 61
    stakes 60
    tactics 56, 60-63
blacksmiths 22, 85
Boucicaut, Marshal 116
bravery 15

castles 12-13, 33, 65, 66-67, 77, 78-91
    concentric 82-83
    crusader 77
    great stone tower 81
    motte and bailey 79

catapults 67
ceremonies 42-43, 44
chapels 79, 84
charging 56-57, 58-59
chivalry 14-29
Christianity 9, 71, 74, 76, 113
coats of arms 51, 102, 117-124
College of Arms 124
courtly love 24-29
crusades 71-77

dancing 41
drawbridges 79, 80
dubbing 43, 44
dungeons 7, 84, 89

Edward, Prince 115
estates 13

fire 67, 70, 79
flails 48
food 85, 87, 89, 90, 91
    tasters 89
foot soldiers 58-59, 60, 63

Galahad, Sir 112
games 91
garderobes 85, 87
Guinevere, Lady 28, 29

hauberks 49
helmets 10, 22, 49
heralds 102-103, 105, 106-107, 117, 124
Holy Grail 110, 112
Holy Land 72, 74, 77
honour 16-19
horses 11, 13, 14, 21, 35, 38, 39, 53, 54, 117
   coursers 54
   destriers 54
   palfreys 54
   riding tips 39
Hospitallers 76, 77
hunting 12, 91

Jerusalem 72
jesters 88
John, King of Bohemia 23
jousts 98-100, 104-105
   tilts 100

kings 30, 43, 110, 117

ladies 24, 25, 27, 41, 75, 100
Lancelot, Sir 28, 29, 111
lances 37-38, 46, 56, 57, 99, 100
lords 13, 33, 35, 65, 90, 94

maces 48
Marshal, William 23, 114
mêlées 94-97
merrelles 91
Middle East 72
military service 32
moats 80
music 91
Muslims 72, 113

nobles 30, 42, 55

orders 52

pages 34
palisades 79
pas d'armes 108

peasants 31
pikes 59
poison 67, 89
pollaxes 47
priests 20, 44, 64, 97
princes 115
prisoners 19, 63, 89, 94

queens 24
quintains 38

raids 64-65
ransoms 63, 94, 114
Rodrigo de Vivar (El Cid) 113

secret exit 84
servants 34
shields 40, 51, 118-123
sieges 66-70
    battering rams 66
    crows 69
    defending against 68-70
    scaling ladders 66

siege towers 66, 70
    trebuchets 67
    tunnels 67, 70
single combat 101
solars 85
spurs 39, 45
squires 34-43, 53
standard bearers 59
swords 10, 35, 40, 43, 45, 46, 47, 97

Templars 75, 76, 77
toilets 67, 85, 87
tournaments 92-105, 114
training 33

wars 32, 55
weapons 36, 37, 40, 46-48, 66-70
wells 85

First published in 1456 by Medieval Manuscripts Limited.
This edition published in 2026 by Usborne Publishing Limited,
83-85 Saffron Hill, London EC1N 8RT, United Kingdom. usborne.com

Copyright ©2026, 2014, 2009, 2005 Usborne Publishing Limited.

The name Usborne and the Balloon logo are registered trade marks of Usborne Publishing Limited. All rights reserved. No part of this publication may be reproduced or used in any manner for the purpose of training artificial intelligence technologies or systems (including for text or data mining), stored in retrieval systems or transmitted in any form or by any means without prior permission of the publisher. Printed in UAE. UKE